COMPUTER KNOWLEDGE

A REFERENCE GUIDE

JERIN THOMAS

XpressPublishing

An imprint of Notion Press

XpressPublishing
An imprint of Notion Press

Old No. 38, New No. 6
McNichols Road, Chetpet
Chennai - 600 031

First Published by Notion Press 2019

ISBN 978-1-64805-447-1

Introduction:

Computers and electronics play an enormous role in today's society, impacting everything from communication and medicine to science.

Although computers are typically viewed as a modern invention involving electronics, computing predates the use of electrical devices. The ancient abacus was perhaps the first digital computing device. Analog computing dates back several millennia as primitive computing devices were used as early as the ancient Greeks and Romans, the most known complex of which being the Antikythera mechanism. Later devices such as the castle clock (1206), slide rule (c. 1624) and Babbage's Difference Engine (1822) are other examples of early mechanical analog computers.

The introduction of electric power in the 19th century led to the rise of electrical and hybrid electro-mechanical devices to carry out both digital (Hollerith punch-card machine) and analog (Bush's differential analyzer) calculation. Telephone switching came to be based on this technology, which led to the development of machines that we would recognize as early computers.

The presentation of the Edison Effect in 1885 provided the theoretical background for electronic devices. Originally in the form of vacuum tubes, electronic components were rapidly integrated into electric devices, revolutionizing radio and later television. It was in computers however, where the full impact of electronics was felt. Analog computers used to calculate ballistics were crucial to the outcome of World War II, and the Colossus and the ENIAC, the two earliest electronic digital computers, were developed during the war.

RAM (Random Access Memory):

RAM is a memory facility which provides space for your computer to read and write data to be accessed by the CPU (central processing unit). When people mention to a computer's memory, they usually mean its RAM. The programs and data that we use are stored in the RAM temporarily so that the processor can access them fast. RAM is used to load and run programs or applications on a computer's are operating system. Extra RAM means more applications and programs can be run simultaneously. The speed is measured in MHz, (or megahertz). The capacity of RAM is measured in bits, bytes, kilobytes, megabytes, gigabytes, terabytes and the typical capacity of RAM in a PC is 512MB to 8GB.

There are other types of RAM which are;

SDRAM (synchronous dram)

DDR(double data ratter)

Rambus Dram (RDRMM)

ROM (Read Only Memory):

Is a class of storage media used in computers and other electronic devices. Data stored in ROM cannot be modified, or can be modified only slowly or with difficulty, so it is mainly used to distribute firmware. The BIOS software is built into the PC, and is the first code run by a PC when powered on ('boot firmware'). The primary function of the BIOS is to load and start an operating system. BIOS software is stored on a non-volatile ROM chip built into the system on the mother board. The first job for the BIOS is to initialize and identify system devices such as the video display card, keyboard and mouse, hard disk, CD/DVD drive and other hardware.

These are the types of ROM:

Mask-Programmed ROM (MROM)

Programmable ROM (PROM)

Erasable-Programmable ROM (EPROM)

Electrically Erasable PROM (EEPROM)

Input devices:

Input devices are any piece of computer hardware equipment used to provide data and give in information to the computer. They allow us to enter the information and data into the computer.E.g.

Mouse:

Is an input device which inputs information by clicking the mouse and being able to move the arrow in the monitor by using the mouse. Mouse can display mainframe data records that contain a leading 4 byte record length counter. With proper options, mouse can add carriage returns to fixed length records.

Types of mouse:

laser mouse

mechanical mouse

cordless mouse

KEYBORAD:

The set of typewriter – like keys that enables you to enter data into a computer. Computer keyboards are similar to electric-typewriter keyboards but contain additional keys. It control the computer and purposes includes a plurality of sets of two or more keys arranged for receiving the tips of the finger of a hand of an operator, the keys of each set have such a small superficial touch area and are clustered together. So as to be substantially comprehended and selectively operated by a single finger tip of an operator. There different types of keyboards:

Ergonomic Keyboards

Wireless keyboards

Illuminated keyboards

Output Devices:

Output Devices are used to communicate the outcomes of data processing carried out by information to the computer to the outside world. Which we get information out of the computer.

E.g.

Printers will print anything that in on that is on the monitor onto paper. This can be pictures, words and numbers.

Monitor

Monitor is a device that displays images or symbols generated by computers, an output device that is a part of your computer display system. They

Serve as the visual display to help you navigate your computer. Also to display text and graphics, produced by a computer. The resolution is the measurement of the number of pixels that a computer displays, also called a computer monitor, can show at one time. Monitors that display more pixels offer a sharper, brighter image. Monitors are measured in inches, diagonally from top left to bottom right.

Types of monitors:

CRT (Cathode Ray Tube) Monitor

LCD (Liquid Crystal Display) Monitor

Printers:

Printer is a peripheral which produces a text and/or graphics) of documents stored in electronic form, usually on physical print media such as paper or transparencies. It lets you to get a hard copy of a document, or picture. DPI (dots per inch) most printer's print 600 dpi printers print 600 tiny little dots across one inch and 600 dots vertically for one inch. The higher the resolution of your printer or image setter, the greater detail you can print and the better appearance of your output. The speed of printers is measured in print-per-minute (PPM) for example, laser printer ratings range from 6 to 15 ppm, inkjets are rated 4 ppm and up for black text, and photo-quality inkjets range from 0.3 to 12 ppm, depending on the job.

Types of printers:

Laser printers

Ink-jet printers

Dot matrix printers

Disk Storage devices (Backing store)

Disk Drives are used to record information from the computer onto a floppy disk or CD.

Hard Disk Drive:

Hard disk drive (HDD) main storage used to permanently store all including the operating system, data, files and programs on the computer. Most hard drives are permanently stored in an internal drive bay at the front of the computer. Capacity per HDD increasing from 3.75 megabytes to greater than 1 terabyte. The typical capacity of hard disk in a PC is uses a 400 to 500 GB drive.

Types of Hard Disk:

Desktop Hard Disk Types: 3.5′, IDE and Sata Interfaces

Laptop Hard Disk Types:2.5′, 1.8′, IDE, Sata, SCSI

Server Hard Disk types:3.5′ Sata, SCSI

Optical Disk Storage CD/DVD/Blu-Ray

CD Disk:

A Compact Disc (CD) is an optical disc used to store digital data. It was originally developed to store sound recordings exclusively, but later it also allowed the preservation of other types of data.It is used to store data, video or music. So that makes it a storage device. A standard CD has a capacity of about 74 minutes of standard CD audio music. There are extended CDs that can actually exceed this limit and pack more than 80 minutes on a disk. CD's are capable of storing up to 700 mb.

The types of CD's are:

CD-ROM is a pre-pressed compact disc that contains data accessible to, but not writable by, a computer for data storage and music playback.

CD-R a CD-R (Compact Disc-Recordable) is a variation of the Compact Disc invented by Philips and Sony. CD-R is a Write Once Read Many (WORM) optical medium, though the whole disk does not have to be entirely written in the same session.

CD-Rewritable disk, a type of CD disk that enables you to write onto it in multiple sessions. One of the problems with CD-R disks is that you can only write to them once.

DVD Disk:

DVD (Digital Video Disc) is an optical disc storage media format, which are of the same dimensions as compact discs (CDs), but are capable of storing almost seven times as much data. The storage capacity of a DVD is approximately 4.7 GB (gigabytes). A dual layer doubles the storage but requires a dual-layer DVD player/recorder to use the dual-layer media.

The types of DVD'S:

DVD-R

DVD-RW

DVD-ROM

Blu-Ray Disk:

Blu-ray Disc is an optical disc storage medium designed to supersede the DVD format. The format defines as its standard physical media a 12 cm (same as DVDs and CDs), 25 GB per-layer optical disc, with dual layer discs (50 GB) the norm for feature-length video discs and additional layers possible later. The capacity of Blu-ray disk is 25 GB (single-layer) 50 GB (dual-layer).

USB Memory Stick

USB flash drives are computer devices that inputs information that is saved on the USB and inputs it in to the computer when you insert the USB. Also typically removable and rewritable, and physically much smaller than a floppy disk. USB drives range in capacity from megabytes up to 256GB and offer much more storage than writable CDs and DVDs.

Operating system

Is software, containing of programs and data, which runs on computers and manages the computer hardware and runs common services for active carrying out of various application software. Operating systems are responsible for everything from the control and allocation of memory to recognizing input from external devices and transmitting output to computer displays. They also manage files on computer hard drives and control peripherals, like printers and scanners. An operating system also has a vital role to play in security. Its job includes preventing unauthorized users from accessing the computer system.

Examples of operating systems:

Windows Vista

Windows 7

About a computer:

A computer is a machine that can be instructed to carry out sequences of arithmetic or logical operations automatically via computer programming. Modern computers have the ability to follow generalized sets of operations, called programs. These programs enable computers to perform an extremely wide range of tasks. A "complete" computer including the hardware, the operating system (main software), and peripheral equipment required and used for "full" operation can be referred to as a computer system. This term may as well be used for a group of computers that are connected and work together, in particular a computer network or computer cluster.

Computers are used as control systems for a wide variety of industrial and consumer devices. This includes simple special purpose devices like microwave ovens and remote controls, factory devices such as industrial robots and computer-aided design, and also general purpose devices like personal computers and mobile devices such as smartphones. The Internet is run on computers and it connects hundreds of millions of other computers and their users.

Early computers were only conceived as calculating devices. Since ancient times, simple manual devices like the abacus aided people in doing calculations. Early in the Industrial Revolution, some mechanical devices were built to automate long tedious tasks, such as guiding patterns for looms. More sophisticated electrical machines did specialized analog calculations in the early 20th century. The first digital electronic calculating machines were developed during World War II. The first semiconductor transistors in the late 1940s were followed by the silicon-based MOSFET (MOS transistor) and monolithic integrated circuit (IC) chip technologies in the late 1950s, leading to the microprocessor and the microcomputer revolution in the 1970s. The speed, power and versatility of computers have been increasing dramatically ever since then, with MOS transistor counts increasing at a rapid pace (as predicted by Moore's law), leading to the Digital Revolution during the late 20th to early 21st centuries.

Conventionally, a modern computer consists of at least one processing element, typically a central processing unit (CPU) in the form of a metal-oxide-semiconductor (MOS) microprocessor, along with some type of computer memory, typically MOS semiconductor memory chips. The processing element carries out arithmetic and logical operations, and a sequencing and control unit can change the order of operations in response to stored information. Peripheral devices include input devices (keyboards, mice, joystick, etc.), output devices (monitor screens, printers, etc.), and input/output devices that perform both functions (e.g., the 2000s-era touchscreen). Peripheral devices allow information to be retrieved from an external source and they enable the result of operations to be saved and retrieved.

Role of computer in business

The use of computers among maximum practiced in the field of business. In fact, small businesses also use the computer as there are now very cheap microcomputers. Business organizations now have a number of facts and a lot of numbers to be processed. So many businesses have started using the computer, for example to calculate the salary, to identify the goods sold and are still in stock, to issue and send or receive business statements, letters, invoices and more.

The use of computers and office equipment to assist other managers, clerks, and the management of office automation mentioned. One of them is a word processing type of electronic method that enables us to produce and edit letters, reports, documents, and other than work in a few seconds to type manually. Many of the office to produce standard letters, such as payment of the balance, invitations and more. In addition, local business organizations to use computers to create, save, and send envoys to a particular place. The advantages of using computers in this area, clearly it is very important in a business organization.

Role of Computers in Banking and Financial

Processing data involving savings accounts, fixed deposits, loans, investments, profitability analysis, and so on are among the organizations operating budget. The measures used are standard and recurrent. And with that, the financial institution is the first user is aware of the importance of computers to save time. Use of financial institutions including electronic fund transfer activities for example a bank has a terminal in each branch in the country and also in supermarkets, petrol stations, schools, factories, homes, hotels, and so on.

The company will move employees' salary into the account by entering employee identification numbers then pay the money transferred into the account supermarkets, hotels, or gas station when making a purchase. Money transfer facility is referred to the electronic transfer of money is very effective use is safe and quick method for financial transactions. With the facility, known as ETC is also individual can issue, transfer, and include cash or checks to the current balance at any time. Clearly the main purpose of the use of computers in financial institutions can assist in arranging the affairs of clients and provide services better and more efficient, reduce fraud in financial transactions also eliminate cash transactions involving the community with the goal to create a cashless society.

Role of Computers in Industrial Areas

Industry is a lot of benefit from the use of computers and the development of a human machine that 'robot'.

Industrial production, for example requires a lot of computers to process data collected from employees, customers, sales, product information, production schedules, and so on. Yes said the computer used to control the production process.

Especially the production of information processing inventory control to keep the latest information about the remaining inventory of raw materials and finished goods used to determine the value of inventory and stock status. This computer can alert the staff involved if he should order the raw materials and when to deliver the goods completed to the customer. Similarly, to store information about the structure of an item, but the material requirement planning processes also use computers to facilitate the work. Appear in the computer industry is very broad and also affect the development of industry in a country.

Role of Computers in Education

Now in this era of science and technology become more advanced, the computer may take over the role of books in the store and disseminate knowledge to the public. In other words, the computer will change the way we learn and the way we store knowledge. Hal-related matters such as student registration, class scheduling, processing of examination results, students 'and teachers' personal storage can be implemented by a computer with a fast and effective in helping the administration. Now exams results were processed by computer. The IPT also the duties of office automation, processing, scientific research results and also use the computer. In fact, cataloging books in libraries also apply to computer use. Last but not least is used for teaching and learning process is not only at institutions of higher learning in the schools, both for teaching and studying computer-assisted education on computer is very emphasized that in the field of education for helping in the administrative process, research is what is important is the ease and help students and teachers in the teaching and learning.

Role of Computers in the Medical

Hospitals and clinics use computers to store patient records, scheduling doctors, nurses and other personnel, inventory and purchase of medicines, medical research and medical diagnosis. Applications of computer-based equipment or use of information technology has help doctors to diagnose diseases. It is clear that the use of computers in the medical field to provide solutions to complex problems. Among the new computer technology that provides assistance to those who are disabled. Microprocessor-based voice systems assist people with disabilities speaking with a terminal that directs the computer to perform a verbal task. Similarly, the development of computers has helped the blind to see, the deaf to communicate, whether with the help of speech synthesizer or using the keyboard. This can be help them become more active and can do what they could not do before. Besides works of traditional data processing, such as issuing bills of patients, medical statistics and scheduling of staff and others have also streamlined and processed by computer.

Hospital Information System that is used can be stored in a centralized patient database. In fact, the use of information technology the computer is programmed to culture and analyze bacteria, viruses, and other infections agents to automatically detect and identify a disease thus enabling the hospitals and laboratories to begin treatment. For example, Computer Help Demography machine (Computer Aided Demography, CAT) used for the purpose. Similarly, computers are used for a patient oversee psychological variables such as blood pressure, body temperature, ECG (Electro-Cardiograph) and sounded a warning if something unusual happens. For this purpose the computer to read different variables and make comparison with standard values. If there is something extraordinary happens the computer will draw the attention of doctors and nurses to issue a warning. Clearly, it was found that the computer has a wide range of accommodation in the medical field.

Role of Computers in Legal

Computers have been used in the legislative process in recent years. The use of the most important is the preparation of documents using a word processor. The use of computer accounting legislation also includes processing to produce weekly and monthly reports, keep records of payments consulting, diary for the latest attorney information consumers about the various court procedures and also to keep records of users. As this area is very complicated, it is the need to retrieve the required information either on journal of law, an important case, scale, and statistics or important decisions for the purpose of making the decision to retain legal data bank. Thus the use of one computer will help lawyers and trainee lawyers and law students find relevant data without wasting time and get better service.

Role of Computers in Government

Government sector is one of the largest users of computer usage practices in implementing administrative matters. All the necessary data can be obtained in a short time such as information about people, services, economic planning, and land development projects and for planning and decision making. Through long-term weather forecasting computer can now be done. With tie loss of life can be because of better information and faster. "The success of Neil Am strong on July 23, 1969 landing on the moon is also made possible with the help of computers used to design spacecraft, space for clothes astronauts, and flight schedules". This shows the very important use of computers in the field of space transportation. Service tax and income tax collection was simplified by using the computer. Keeping records of taxpayers who do it manually, and bring many problems have been addressed with the use of computer and services can make the task more efficiently and quickly.

Similarly, in the military, use of computer store inventory held until the war simulation on the screen. Computers are also used to follow the movement of the enemy in the border areas. Traffic flow can be managed effectively by detecting the direction of traffic using the many tools of detection. In this way, if there are more vehicles from one direction, the computer will let the green light goes on for a suitable period of time. "In the field of transport, Cosmos- 11 introduced by Mass by providing facilities for passengers to know the status including those booking hotel reservations, from anywhere in the world". Similarly, business owners and vehicle registration can be performed with the use of computers. Many of the all administrative affairs are managed by using the computer. This not only saves time but can do all things more practical.

Role of Computers in entertainment

Now the computer can be programmed to play music. Places of entertainment with music controlled by computer are cheaper and can be used at any time. Computers are also used to arrange the order of dance and music. Each game requires movement. Movement can best be obtained by detailed analysis of a physical system. Computers also can be programmed to depict images of high quality. Drawing using the computer speeds up the process of creating. The work of art can be done and made a review in a short time compared with traditional Kedah. Cartoon films produced by computers have grown so widely.

Role of Computers at daily life

Microcomputer use also home to control the safety and control of air conditioning and lighting. The use of computers in the home allows housewife get the latest information about fashion and can make orders to use supermarket with and video. In addition to budget planning and inventory at home. This is all to do with a microcomputer that is connected to the national data bank. Children can use computers to learn school subjects or educational games. But it is clear that computers have become machines of information in our society.

History of Computers

It is very difficult to find the exact origin of computers. But according to some experts computer exists at the time of world war-II. Also, at that time they were used for keeping data. But, it was for only government use and not for public use. Above all, in the beginning, the computer was a very large and heavy machine.

Working of a Computer

The computer runs on a three-step cycle namely input, process, and output. Also, the computer follows this cycle in every process it was asked to do. In simple words, the process can be explained in this way. The data which we feed into the computer is input, the work CPU do is process and the result which the computer give is output.

Components and Types of Computer

The simple computer basically consists of CPU, monitor, mouse, and keyboard. Also, there are hundreds of other computer parts that can be attached to it. These other parts include a printer, laser pen, scanner, etc.

The computer is categorized into many different types like supercomputers, mainframes, personal computers (desktop), PDAs, laptop, etc. The mobile phone is also a type of computer because it fulfills all the criteria of being a computer.

Get the huge list of more than 500 Essay Topics and Ideas

Uses of Computer in Various Fields

As the usage of computer increased it became a necessity for almost every field to use computers for their operations. Also, they have made working and sorting things easier. Below we are mentioning some of the important fields that use a computer in their daily operation.

Medical Field

They use computers to diagnose diseases, run tests and for finding the cure for deadly diseases. Also, they are able to find a cure for many diseases because of computers.

Research

Whether it's scientific research, space research or any social research computers help in all of them. Also, due to them, we are able to keep a check on the environment, space, and society. Space research helped us to explore the galaxies. While scientific research has helped us to locate resources and various other useful resources from the earth.

Defense

For any country, his defence is most important for the safety and security of its people. Also, computer in this field helps the country's security agencies to detect a threat which can be harmful in the future. Above all the defense industry use them to keep surveillance on our enemy.

Threats from a Computer

Computers have become a necessity also, they have become a threat too. This is due to hackers who steal your private data and leak them on internet. Also, anyone can access this data. Apart from that, there are other threats like viruses, spams, bug and many other problems.

Components Of Computer:

Access to information: Computers are a device that can be used to access the internet and wide range of information for a variety of purposes

Prepare for projects: Computers are essential to prepare for school and college projects and for work reports

Typing and Editing: It helps us type and edit a lot of documents beginning with letters to family to notices, projects and variety of lists and documents

Learning: Computer assisted learning has come to become a tool for learning and has come to revolutionise the ways in which we learn

Distance Education: It is an important requirement for distance education beginning from MOOC courses to correspondence degrees

Instant access to news: The news about various happenings are instantly updated on the internet and can be accessed by the computer

Stay updated: It helps us stay updated about anything and everything from international news to celebrity activities

Connect with people: It helps us stay connected with people through mails, chat rooms and social media

Access social media: We can access social media sites like Facebook, twitter and instagram

Employment and work from home: It provides us access to part time employment such as freelancing and work from home options

Online transactions: We can carry out hassle free transactions through the computer and make payments anywhere and at any time

Shopping: Online shopping is emerging as one of the modes of shopping and the computer enables us to access a variety of products with literally a click of the mouse

Bookings and reservations: A computer helps in making bookings and reservations for travel, parties, movies and a various other events

Variety of applications: The computer comes with a variety of applications that come handy in our day to day life

Budgeting: It's an effective budgeting tool and has software that help in maintaining and developing monthly budgets

Scheduling and lists: It is a good tool for making schedules and keeping lists and with timely updates help us keep on track with our work

Storing personal information digitally: We can store a lot of personal information, pictures and so on digitally on the computer and access it instantly

Leisure: They are also a part of our general leisure time activity including a variety of options like games, educational videos, movies, social media and general surfing of the web

Gaming: Gaming is something that appeals to all ages and one of the most important uses of the computer

Entertainment: It is a source for entertainment like movies, music and so on

Computers are a basic necessity in today's world. We can perform a variety of functions using the computer and it is indeed the technology for the future. From managing our finances or making purchases, it has proved to be a very handy device that has transformed the ways in which we operate in society.

Uses of Computer at Home

Computer can be used at home in the following ways.

Home Budget

Computer can be used to manage Home Budget. You can easily calculate your expenses and income. You can list all expenses in one column and income in another column. Then you can apply any calculation on these columns to plan your home budget. There are also specialize software that can manage your income and expenses and generate some cool reports.

Computer Games

An important use of computers at home is playing games. Different types of games areavailable. These games are a source of entertainment and recreation. Many games areavailable that are specially developed to improve your mental capability and thinking power.

Working from Home

People can manage the office work at home. The owner of a company can check the work of the employees from home. He can control his office while sitting at home.

CONCLUSION

The rapid development of science and technology has changed the pattern of life now. Everything, processing, gathering information, or any aspects of the various areas that were previously done manually, which gives a lot of risk has to be made more effective, faster, and more practical with the application or use of information technology or computer. Covering the use in various fields including business, financial institutions, industry, education, administration and other fields have the desire to realize develop each country. The fact is, computers have become the heart and backbone of society today. Whatever the field, computing has a lot of people taken over the task. It will not only help in the calculations, store information, detect a decision also to increase efficiency and productivity. But they said it is now clear that the use of computers has been widely practiced and used. In line with globalization and the borderless world, the computer is a machine in the information society is also the main artery of all machinery administration in any field.

"Computer Is Not a Device It Is Our Cloud Brain"

-M.
Jerinthomas

Contents